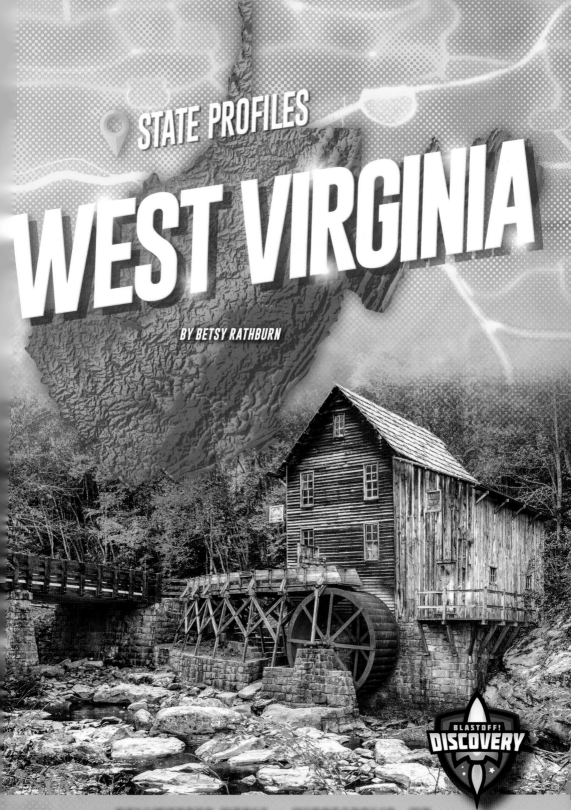

WEST VIRGINIA

BY BETSY RATHBURN

BLASTOFF! DISCOVERY

BELLWETHER MEDIA • MINNEAPOLIS, MN

Blastoff! Discovery launches a new mission: reading to learn. Filled with facts and features, each book offers you an exciting new world to explore!

BLASTOFF! UNIVERSE

BLASTOFF!
Beginners

GRADE
K

BLASTOFF!
READERS

GRADES
1-3

BLASTOFF!
DISCOVERY

GRADE
4

This edition first published in 2022 by Bellwether Media, Inc.

No part of this publication may be reproduced in whole or in part without written permission of the publisher.
For information regarding permission, write to Bellwether Media, Inc.,
Attention: Permissions Department,
6012 Blue Circle Drive, Minnetonka, MN 55343.

Library of Congress Cataloging-in-Publication Data

Names: Rathburn, Betsy, author.
Title: West Virginia / by Betsy Rathburn.
Description: Minneapolis, MN : Bellwether Media, Inc., 2022. |
  Series: Blastoff! Discovery: State profiles | Includes bibliographical
  references and index. | Audience: Ages 7-13 | Audience: Grades 4-6 |
  Summary: "Engaging images accompany information about West Virginia.
  The combination of high-interest subject matter and narrative text is
  intended for students in grades 3 through 8"– Provided by publisher.
Identifiers: LCCN 2021020854 (print) | LCCN 2021020855 (ebook) |
  ISBN 9781644873557 (library binding) | ISBN 9781648341984 (ebook)
Subjects: LCSH: West Virginia–Juvenile literature.
Classification: LCC F241.3 .R37 2022 (print) | LCC F241.3 (ebook) |
  DDC 975.4–dc23
LC record available at https://lccn.loc.gov/2021020854
LC ebook record available at https://lccn.loc.gov/2021020855

Editor: Kate Moening   Designer: Jeffrey Kollock

Printed in the United States of America, North Mankato, MN.

TABLE OF CONTENTS

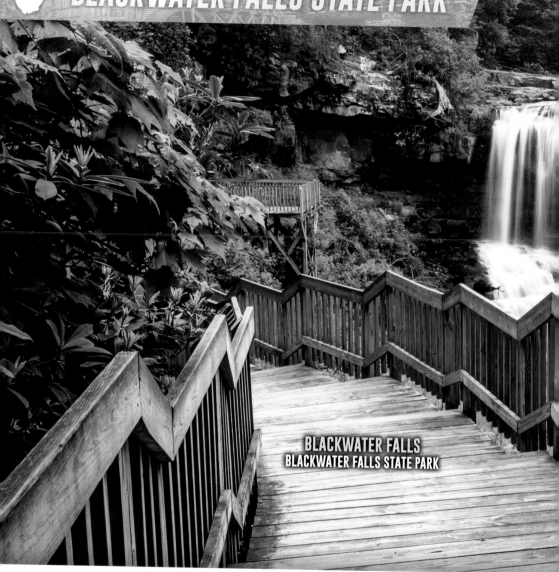

BLACKWATER FALLS
BLACKWATER FALLS STATE PARK

Time to hike! A family follows a trail through Blackwater Falls State Park. Hemlock and red spruce trees line the path. Eastern bluebirds and wood thrushes chirp in the branches. Soon, Blackwater Falls comes into view. The family stops to take pictures of the 57-foot (17-meter) waterfall.

GREEN BANK OBSERVATORY

HARPERS FERRY NATIONAL HISTORICAL PARK

NEW RIVER GORGE NATIONAL PARK

SENECA ROCKS

NEEDLE NAME

Blackwater Falls is named for the dark color of its water. The color comes from hemlock and red spruce needles!

Later, they hike to Elakala Falls. The waterfalls spill down toward the Blackwater River. After their day of hiking is over, the family heads back to their campsite. Tomorrow, they will go fishing on Pendleton Lake. West Virginia is full of fun and nature!

West Virginia is in the eastern United States. It covers 24,230 square miles (62,755 square kilometers). It is the 10th smallest state. The state has two panhandles. The northern panhandle is between Ohio to the west and Pennsylvania to the east. The eastern panhandle is bordered by Maryland to the north and Virginia to the south. Kentucky is West Virginia's southwestern neighbor.

West Virginia has many rivers. The Ohio River follows the state's western border. The Elk and Kanawha Rivers meet in the southwest. Charleston, the state capital, stands where they connect.

OHIO

KANAWHA RIVER

HUNTINGTON

CHARLESTO

KENTUCKY

OHIO
RIVER

PENNSYLVANIA

● WHEELING

MARYLAND

● MORGANTOWN

WEST
VIRGINIA

ELK
RIVER

LACK OF LAKES

Most of West Virginia's lakes
are human-made. Trout Pond
is the state's only natural lake.
It is in the eastern panhandle.

VIRGINIA

N
W + E
S

**BATTLE OF PHILIPPI
CIVIL WAR**

ANCIENT PAST

Starting around 1000 BCE, West Virginia was home to the Adena and then Hopewell peoples. These groups built huge mounds of earth to bury their dead. Some mounds are still visible today!

People have lived in West Virginia for at least 14,000 years. The Fort Ancient people rose around 1000 CE. By 1700, the Shawnee, Iroquois, and other groups had taken over. They used the lands for hunting.

In the 1670s, Europeans claimed the area for the **colony** of Virginia. They began wiping out nearly all Native Americans. After the **Revolutionary War**, Virginia became a state. In the 1860s, it joined the **Confederacy** during the **Civil War**. But western Virginians did not want to leave the U.S. They **seceded** from Virginia in 1861. Two years later, West Virginia became the 35th state.

NATIVE PEOPLES OF WEST VIRGINIA

IROQUOIS CONFEDERACY

- Original lands in north-central West Virginia
- A group of six separate nations: Seneca, Oneida, Tuscarora, Cayuga, Onondaga, and Mohawk
- Also called Haudenosaunee Confederacy and Six Nations

CHEROKEE

- Original lands in western West Virginia
- Descendants largely in the Cherokee Nation of Oklahoma and the Qualla Boundary in North Carolina
- Also called Keetoowah and Aniyunwiya

SHAWNEE

- Original lands in northern West Virginia
- Descendants largely in Oklahoma
- A group of five separate nations: Chalahgawtha, Mekoche, Kispoko, Pekowi, and Hathawekela

DELAWARE

- Original lands in the eastern West Virginia panhandle
- Descendants largely in Oklahoma
- Also called Lenape

The Appalachian Mountains cover all of West Virginia. This mountain chain is made up of many peaks. West Virginia's tallest mountain is Spruce Knob. It is 4,863 feet (1,482 kilometers) high! The Appalachian **Plateau** covers western West Virginia. Many of the state's largest cities are here.

POTOMAC RIVER

SPRUCE KNOB

N
W　E
S

APPALACHIAN PLATEAU

NEW RIVER GORGE
APPALACHIAN MOUNTAINS

LOWEST POINT

West Virginia's lowest point is along the Potomac River. It is only 247 feet (75 meters) above sea level!

SANDSTONE FALLS
NEW RIVER

SPRING
HIGH: 64°F (18°C)
LOW: 41°F (5°C)

SUMMER
HIGH: 82°F (28°C)
LOW: 60°F (16°C)

FALL
HIGH: 65°F (18°C)
LOW: 43°F (6°C)

WINTER
HIGH: 44°F (7°C)
LOW: 24°F (-4°C)

°F = degrees Fahrenheit
°C = degrees Celsius

Most of West Virginia has a **continental** climate. Summers are hot and **humid**, while winters are cold. Spring rains can bring flooding. West Virginia's eastern panhandle gets cool breezes from the Atlantic Ocean. Summers are cooler there than other regions.

West Virginia's skies are home to many animals. Cardinals, sparrows, and blue jays fly throughout the state. At night, great horned owls swoop through West Virginia's forests. Flying squirrels are also active at night. They glide between trees.

Other animals stay on the ground. Bobcats hunt in West Virginia's mountains and forests. White-tailed deer stay quiet to avoid them. Cottontail rabbits and gray squirrels scurry through forests and yards. Salamanders and spotted turtles live in West Virginia's rivers. They swim among pike, bass, and trout!

GREAT HORNED OWL

SOUTHERN FLYING SQUIRREL

WHITE-TAILED DEER

SPOTTED TURTLE

NORTHERN PIKE

BOBCAT

Life Span: up to 15 years
Status: least concern

bobcat range =

LEAST CONCERN	NEAR THREATENED	VULNERABLE	ENDANGERED	CRITICALLY ENDANGERED	EXTINCT IN THE WILD	EXTINCT

PEOPLE AND COMMUNITIES

Nearly 1.8 million people live in West Virginia. Some live in cities such as Charleston, Huntington, or Morgantown. About half of West Virginians live in **rural** areas.

WEST VIRGINIA'S FUTURE: LOSING PEOPLE

West Virginia's population is getting smaller. Many young people leave the state to pursue education and jobs. If the government can draw more people to the state, it could help the problem and improve West Virginia's economy.

RURAL FARMLAND

FAMOUS WEST VIRGINIAN

Name: Brad Paisley
Born: October 28, 1972
Hometown: Glen Dale, West Virginia
Famous For: Country music singer and songwriter who has sold more than 10 million albums and won three Grammy Awards

Most West Virginians have **ancestors** from Europe. Black or African Americans make up the next-largest group. Smaller numbers of Asian Americans, Native Americans, and Hispanic Americans also live in the state. Some West Virginians were born outside of the United States. Many newcomers are from Mexico, Germany, India, and China.

Charleston was founded in the late 1700s. Early on, it was an important place for salt mining. **Steamboats** traveled on West Virginia's rivers to pick up salt. The boats used coal for fuel. Over time, coal mining became more important than salt mining. Charleston has been West Virginia's capital since 1885.

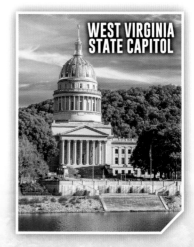

WEST VIRGINIA STATE CAPITOL

CLAY CENTER FOR THE ARTS AND SCIENCES

Today, around 46,000 people live in Charleston. The city is a **cultural** center. People explore shops and restaurants along Capitol Street. On Magic Island, families walk along trails and visit the splash pad. People visit the Clay Center for the Arts and Sciences to see performances and explore the museum.

COAL MINE
PHILIPPI

West Virginia is rich in **natural resources**. Coal mining has been important to the economy since the 1800s. Mines are mostly in the north and southwest. But demand for coal is slowing. Coal pollutes the air and increases climate change. The state is working to grow **tourism** and clean energy industries.

Silica is another natural resource found in West Virginia. This material is used to make glass. Wheeling has been a center for glassmaking since the 1830s. Factory workers also make chemicals, lumber, and metal products. Most West Virginians have **service jobs**. They work in places like schools or hotels.

INVENTED IN WEST VIRGINIA

MOTHER'S DAY

Date Invented: 1907
Inventor: Anna Jarvis

FIRST BRICK ROAD IN U.S.

Date Invented: 1870
Inventor: Mordecai Levi

FIRST STATE SALES TAX

Date Invented: 1921
Started by: West Virginia state legislature

GOLDEN DELICIOUS APPLE

Date Invented: 1912
Inventor: Anderson Mullins

BISCUITS AND GRAVY

West Virginians have many favorite foods. One of their most famous dishes is the pepperoni roll. These soft rolls have pepperoni baked inside. For breakfast, many people enjoy biscuits and gravy. They pour creamy white gravy over fluffy biscuits.

INTO THE MINES

Pepperoni rolls first became popular with Italian miners in the early 1900s. The rolls were easy to take underground!

West Virginians often serve cornbread with beans. Hot dogs have chili and coleslaw on top. In spring and summer, many West Virginians hunt the forests and mountains for wild onions called ramps. In the fall, **venison** is a popular food. The fall apple season inspires many desserts. People bake pies with Golden Delicious apples!

RAMPS

VENISON

PEPPERONI ROLLS

12 SERVINGS

Have an adult help you make this tasty recipe!

INGREDIENTS

1 package of premade bread rolls, unbaked

1 package of pepperoni

DIRECTIONS

1. Preheat the oven to 350 degrees Fahrenheit (177 degrees Celsius).

2. Flatten each thawed roll into a 6-inch (15-centimeter) square.

3. Lay a row of pepperoni in the middle of the dough. Lay another row of slices next to the first.

4. Roll the dough around the pepperoni. Pinch the ends closed and place on a baking sheet. Repeat until the baking sheet is full.

5. Bake for 30 to 35 minutes or until golden brown.

Camping and fishing are common in West Virginia's parks. People enjoy hiking on the state's many mountain trails. Hunting is a popular activity in the fall. Winter brings skiers to the state's mountain slopes. People head to West Virginia's cities to visit museums, go shopping, or see live performances.

HIKING

NOTABLE SPORTS TEAM

West Virginia Mountaineers

Sport: National Collegiate Athletic Association Division I football

Started: 1891

Place of Play: Mountaineer Field at Milan Puskar Stadium

West Virginians love sports. Many football fans root for the University of West Virginia Mountaineers. The West Virginia Black Bears and West Virginia Power draw baseball fans to their games. West Virginians also like to watch and play basketball, ice hockey, and soccer.

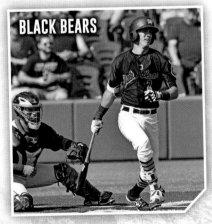

BLACK BEARS

Many festivals celebrate West Virginia's culture. Each May, Buckhannon's West Virginia Strawberry Festival honors strawberry growers. The celebration includes strawberry treats, art, and a parade! The West Virginia Black **Heritage** Festival takes place in September. People gather to watch live music and take part in a **block party**.

Music and art are important to West Virginians. The Vandalia Gathering draws many visitors each spring. People eat, browse art, and listen to live music. In the fall, the Mountain Heritage Arts & Crafts Festival is full of handmade crafts. West Virginians have a lot to celebrate!

MOTHMAN

The Mothman Festival honors a mysterious creature said to haunt Point Pleasant, West Virginia. People gather to enjoy costumes, music, and hayrides!

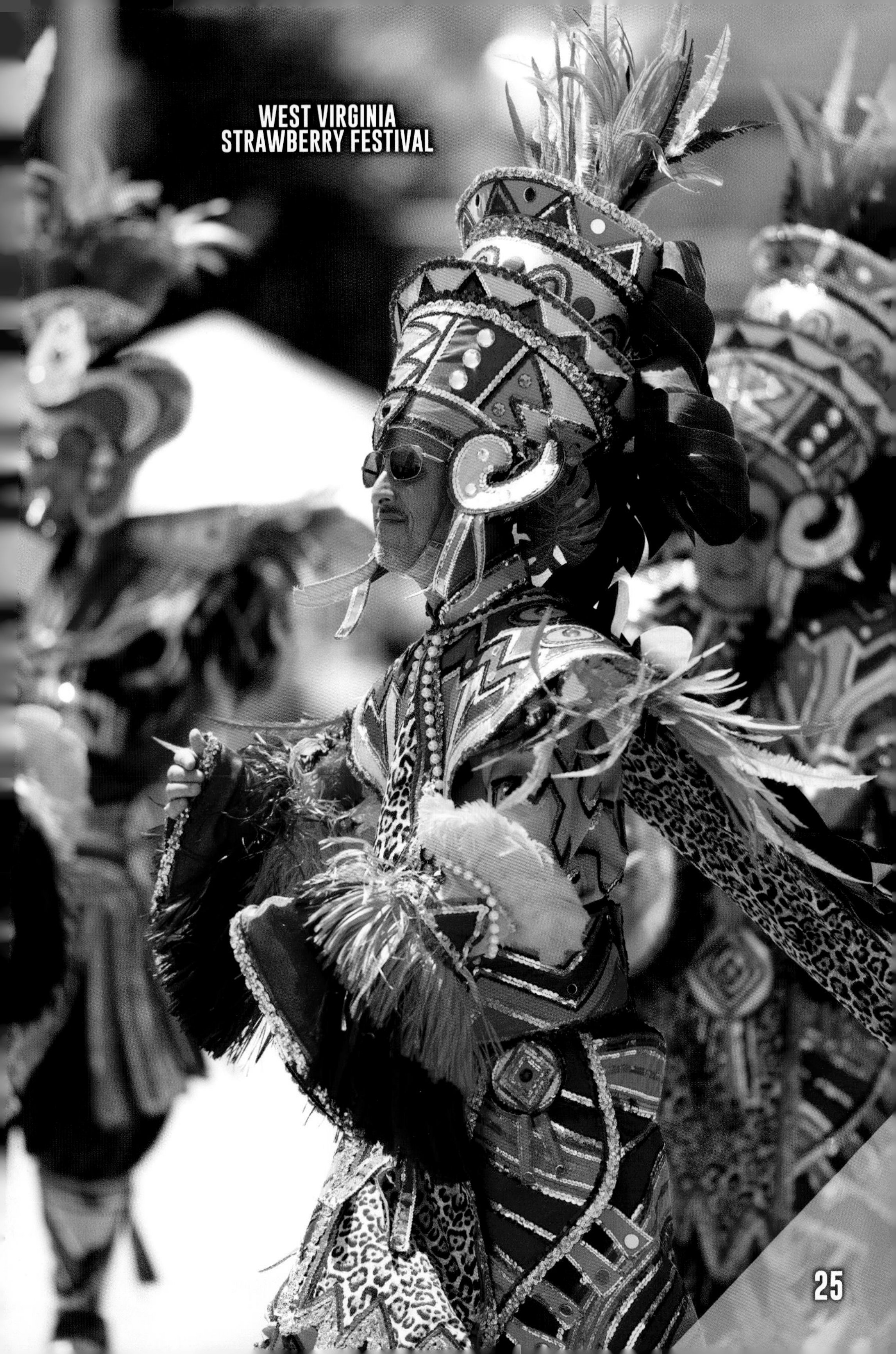
WEST VIRGINIA
STRAWBERRY FESTIVAL

AROUND 1650

Iroquois force the Fort Ancient people out of what is now West Virginia

1859

Anti-slavery activist John Brown attacks Harpers Ferry, a major event that helps lead to the Civil War

1742

John P. Salling discovers coal on the Coal River

1670s

The first Europeans arrive in West Virginia

1861

West Virginia votes to separate from Virginia to join the Union in the Civil War

1774

The Treaty of Camp Charlotte forces the Shawnee to lose control of their land south of the Ohio River

1863

West Virginia becomes the 35th state

2016

In June, major flooding causes deaths and destroys hundreds of homes

1928

Minnie Buckingham Harper becomes the first Black woman to serve in a state legislature

2010

The Upper Big Branch mine explosion is the worst mine disaster in many years

1912

West Virginia coal miners begin demanding better conditions in what becomes known as the Coal Wars

Nickname: The Mountain State

Motto: *Montani semper liberi,* Latin for "Mountaineers Are Always Free."

Date of Statehood: June 20, 1863 (the 35th state)

Capital City: Charleston ★

Other Major Cities: Huntington, Morgantown, Parkersburg, Wheeling

Area: 24,230 square miles (62,755 square kilometers); West Virginia is the 41st largest state.

Population

1,793,716 (2020)

STATE FLAG

West Virginia's flag is white with a dark blue border. At the center of the flag is a large yellow shield. Inside the shield are a farmer and a miner. They stand next to a rock that says "June 20, 1863," the date of West Virginia's statehood. Above the shield is a banner that reads "State of West Virginia." Around the shield are two rhododendrons, the state flower of West Virginia.

INDUSTRY

Main Exports

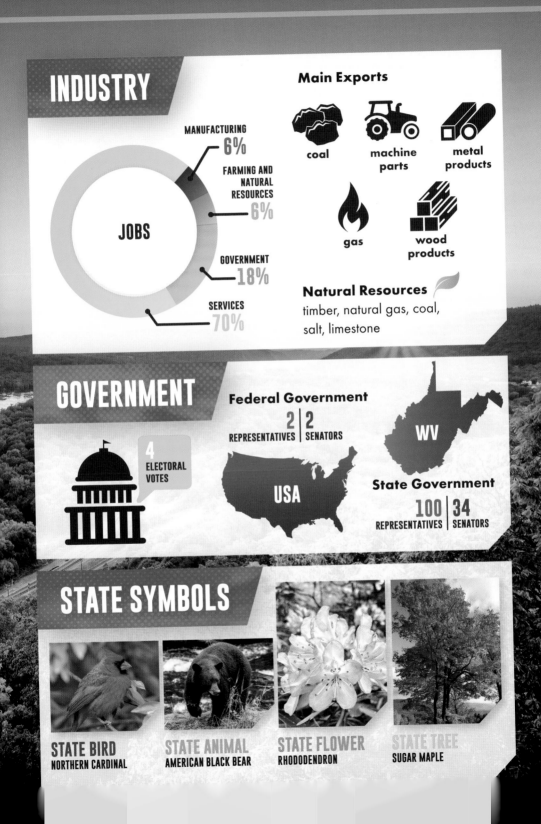

JOBS

- MANUFACTURING **6%**
- FARMING AND NATURAL RESOURCES **6%**
- GOVERNMENT **18%**
- SERVICES **70%**

coal

machine parts

metal products

gas

wood products

Natural Resources
timber, natural gas, coal, salt, limestone

GOVERNMENT

Federal Government

2 REPRESENTATIVES | **2** SENATORS

4 ELECTORAL VOTES

USA

WV

State Government

100 REPRESENTATIVES | **34** SENATORS

STATE SYMBOLS

STATE BIRD
NORTHERN CARDINAL

STATE ANIMAL
AMERICAN BLACK BEAR

STATE FLOWER
RHODODENDRON

STATE TREE
SUGAR MAPLE

GLOSSARY

ancestors—relatives who lived long ago

block party—an outdoor party put on by the residents of a neighborhood

Civil War—a war between the Northern (Union) and Southern (Confederate) states that lasted from 1861 to 1865

colony—a distant territory which is under the control of another nation

Confederacy—the group of southern states that formed a new country in the early 1860s; the Confederacy fought against the Northern states during the Civil War.

continental—referring to a climate that has hot summers and cold winters, such as those found in central North America and Asia

cultural—relating to the beliefs, arts, and ways of life in a place or society

heritage—the traditions, achievements, and beliefs that are part of the history of a group of people

humid—having a lot of moisture in the air

natural resources—materials in the earth that are taken out and used to make products or fuel

plateau—an area of flat, raised land

Revolutionary War—the war from 1775 to 1783 in which the United States fought for independence from Great Britain

rural—related to the countryside

seceded—officially withdrew from a nation or state

service jobs—jobs that perform tasks for people or businesses

silica—a hard mineral found in sand and some rocks

steamboats—boats powered by steam engines; steam engines are engines that generate power with steam.

tourism—the business of people traveling to visit other places

venison—meat from a deer

TO LEARN MORE

AT THE LIBRARY

Kaminski, Leah. *West Virginia Mountaineers*. New York, N.Y.: AV2 by Weigl, 2020.

Schwabacher, Martin. *West Virginia*. New York, N.Y.: Children's Press, 2019.

Tieck, Sarah. *West Virginia*. Minneapolis, Minn.: Big Buddy Books, 2020.

ON THE WEB

FACTSURFER

Factsurfer.com gives you a safe, fun way to find more information.

1. Go to www.factsurfer.com.

2. Enter "West Virginia" into the search box and click 🔍.

3. Select your book cover to see a list of related content.

INDEX